NOSEPICKING
⇥ FOR ⇤
PLEASURE

NOSEPICKING

⟞ FOR ⟝

PLEASURE

A HANDY GUIDE
by
ROLAND FLICKET

Picktorially Illustrated
by JON HIGHAM

MICHAEL O'MARA BOOKS LIMITED

First published in Great Britain
by Little, Brown and Company in 1992

This updated edition published in 2007 by
Michael O'Mara Books Limited
9 Lion Yard, Tremadoc Road
London sw4 7nq

Papers used by Michael O'Mara Books Limited are natural,
recyclable products made from wood grown in sustainable forests.
The manufacturing processes conform to the environmental
regulations of the country of origin.

ISBN 978-1-84317-268-0

3 5 7 9 10 8 6 4 2

www.mombooks.com

Designed and typeset by Martin Bristow

Printed and bound in Great Britain by Cox & Wyman,
Reading, Berks

Contents

About the Author and Illustrator   6

Acknowledgements   7

Introduction   9

1 A Brief History of Nosepicking   11

2 Nosepicking – Your Questions Answered   43

3 P.Y.O. – The Technique of Nosepicking   73

4 Problems with Picking   83

5 A Fun Fact File for Pickers   89

6 Nostrildamus – Your Future in the Stars   95

7 Nosepicking in Art   111

8 Nosepicking in Verse and Song   117

Glossary of Terms   125

ABOUT THE AUTHOR

ROLAND FLICKET is acknowledged as one of the world's leading authorities on nosepicking. He was born in 1934 in Pittsburgh, Pennsylvania. His interest in rhinology developed at an early age when he won the Hanky Memorial Prize at Greenball High School. After studying medicine at the University of St Cilium he moved to Los Angeles to make an intensive study of nosepickers. *Follicle and Phlegm* was the result, a seminal work that plucked nasal hair from obscurity to the top of the rhinology agenda for the first time. He followed this in 1976 with *A Bridge Too Far*. A far-reaching article, 'Cotton Buds – Whither?', published in the British medical journal *The Lancet* in 1979, brought him further acclaim. *Drip, Tip and Lip*, an examination of nose-blowing worldwide, appeared in 1989. In 2002 he was awarded the Conkressional Medal, America's highest honour for nosepickers. Roland Flicket is Emeritus Professor of Nasal Archaeology at his alma mater and is currently Visiting a Fellow at Brasenose College, Oxford. He is married with one son, also an enthusiastic nosepicker.

ABOUT THE ILLUSTRATOR

JON HIGHAM has an unrivalled reputation as an illustrator of children's books. *Piddling In The Po*, *Frumpy Fergie's Frolics* and the *Gertie Goldfish Goes Into . . .* series are some of his bestselling titles. He studied at the Norwich School for Nasal Artists and now lives in Battle with his wife and daughter, dog Snot and a thirty-four-year-old tortoise called Squit.

Acknowledgements

I am deeply grateful to a large number of friends and acquaintances who have helped me with the research for this book. The long hours spent picking their noses in my company have been of inestimable value and I thank them.

I am under an obligation to my colleagues, the staff and students at the University of St Cilium for their understanding and goodwill; Jon Higham for the accuracy and detail of his superb illustrations; Bram Tatorus ('Seer To The Stars') of the *Los Angeles Argus* for his study of Nostrildamus; my publishers and the many others who continue to fight with me for the rights of nosepickers; the late Mr. C. de Bergerac, President of the International Conkress of Competitive Nosepicking; and finally, my wife SheriLee Flicket for typing the manuscript, and my son Adam Zachary for the lyrics and music of the song 'March of the Nosepickers' (see p. 119), and for supplying much unsolicited material.

Roland Flicket
University of St Cilium,
California

Introduction

NOSEPICKING is man's most popular pastime – and the oldest. Considering this, remarkably little has been written on the subject. With a growing number of traffic wardens, snooker players and mobile-phone users, nosepicking is on the increase. Yet government legislation to ban all nosepicking in restaurants, cars and post offices is imminent. Nosepickers' freedoms are again under threat and snot is once more on the menu.

Roland Flicket is the world's leading authority on bogies. With this handy guide he strikes a blow for nosepickers everywhere. Already translated into six languages, *Nosepicking for Pleasure* charts the history of nosepicking through the

centuries, traces the development of its technique and contains a wide range of advice for pickers on every aspect of picking, rolling and flicking.

If you haven't yet discovered the joys of picking your nose, this comprehensive volume will provide a blow-by-blow intro-duction; if you are a confirmed nosepicker, the tips and refinements distilled from Professor Flicket's long experience will surely add to your enjoyment and make picking an even greater pleasure.

'All the fun of sex without the risks.'

1
A Brief History of Nosepicking

SINCE time immemorial, Man* has picked his nose. But it was not until the Kung Flu epidemic of 985 BC that nosepicking was raised to an art form. For the first time in recorded history, there was enough snot everywhere for artists and explorers to pick to their heart's content. Ideas were exchanged, new routes were opened up, techniques were developed and the beginnings of nosepicking as we know it today were carved out.

Nevertheless, evidence of the origins of nosepicking, shrouded in the mists of time, stretch back yet further. The earliest pictorial documentation we have shows that as early as 4,075 BC nosepicking was deeply embedded in the culture of the Ancient Egyptians.

*But not Woman. Well, have you ever met one who did it? (R. F.)

Hieroglyphics over 6,000 years old decorate the tomb of the Egyptian Boy-King Pik'n-likun. The young Pharaoh is depicted on the various stages of his journey to the Underworld, wearing on his head the small cotton square, ancient symbol of monarchy. Today, we call that same square of cotton a 'handkerchief' and, although not used for its original purpose nowadays, it is still worn on the head in some areas of the British Isles and on the Costa Brava.

Pik'n-likun's ornately decorated coffin was not discovered until 1921, and when the coffin was opened, the mummified body of Pik'n-likun was seen exactly as it had been laid to rest sixty centuries before, miraculously preserved.

CARBON-DATING TECHNIQUES

Scientists were even able to determine that, at the time of his burial, the Pharaoh, in common with most boys of his age, had needed a clean handkerchief. (Carbon dating of the bogies was put at 4,100–3,500 BC.)

The nosepicking skills developed by the Ancient Egyptians were passed on hand to mouth from generation to generation, spreading to all corners of the modern world. The first reference to the habit in Britain is found in the journals of the Roman general Mucus Maximus, who commanded a garrison in the north of England about AD 198.

NECESSE MIHI FVIT REPREHENDERE
PROBOSCIDEM, MILITEM QVARTAE
DECIMAE COHORTIS, QVOD SECVNDA
VIGILIA NOCTIS SVB ARMIS NASVM
VELLISSET. 'DECET MILITEM ROMANVM'
INQVAM, 'IVSSIS IMPERATORIS PARERE
ET TOGA VTI.' SED REM NON REFERAM.
QVAMQVAM MATREM SVAM DESIDERAT,
PROBOSCIS ET VIR PRAECLARISSIMVS
ET LEGIONI HONORI EST.

I had cause to reprimand Proboscis, soldier of the XIVth cohort, for picking his nose in uniform and while keeping the second watch. 'A soldier of Rome should obey the orders of his Emperor,' quoth I, 'and use his toga.' This incident I shall not report for, although he misses his mother, Proboscis is a fine boy and a credit to the Legion.

Mucus was but one of a stream of Roman commanders charged by his Emperor to keep the marauding Pickts and Snots from breaching the defences of Hadrian's Wall. It was not, however, till some 600 years after the Romans finally left Britain that nosepicking began to play an important part in the country's history.

It came about as a result of the Battle of Hastings in 1066. King Harold, an inveterate nosepicker, did much to encourage the habit in Wessex and Mercia during his reign. Alas, it was his undoing. While directing his troops at the Battle of Hastings, Harold became preoccupied with a large nasal deposit while sitting astride his horse and was picked off by a Norman archer. The scene was woven into the Bayeux Tapestry.

As a result of Harold's disastrous loss of concentration, Duke William of Normandy won the battle and the English Crown, thus changing the course of history. Nosepicking in public was banned by royal decree and ruthlessly suppressed. Offenders were sentenced to death, dispatched in a single blow by the dreaded Pick-axe.

Furthermore, lest any soldier should be tempted to stick his finger up his nose while waiting to do battle, the chain-mail glove was developed. This act, known as the Decree Nosi, had a profound effect on the next 400 years or so and is largely responsible for the slow development of nosepicking in the British Isles while other nations were forging ahead. The act earned the Norman King the nickname 'William the Conk' and is held by historians to be the principal reason for the string of French military successes over the following centuries. This is reflected in the motto adapted by the army at the time and still proudly used today: *Nemo me impune lacessit* ('No one picks my nose and gets away with it').

It was during the reign of King John that the problems caused by the repressive Decree Nosi first surfaced. The earls and barons, who had so nobly supported the monarchy in its various armed causes, felt that, in return, nosepicking rights should be restored to them. For over 200 years this request had been refused by successive kings. The situation altered radically when John came to the throne, for he continued to deny the earls and barons their rights while being a compulsive, obsessive nosepicker himself. Rarely seen in public without a finger up his nose, it was too much for the earls and barons.

Feelings ran so strong that, in a display of strength and unity rare in English history, the earls and barons joined together and forced King John to agree to let them pick their noses whenever they pleased. In 1215, the great Magna Carta was signed by the King at Runnynose guaranteeing the earls and barons the right to:

> Picke in perpetuitie ye noble nose, whether it be in ye market place or in fair ladye's chamber, in ye castle turret or in ye banquet hall; for he today that picks his nose with me shall be my brother; be he ne'er so vile, this day shall gentle his condition; and gentlemen in England now abed shall think themselves accursed they were not here and hold their manhoods cheap whiles any speak that picked his nose upon Saint Crispin's day.

It was a victory for the rulers of the country, who were now able to pick their noses whenever they pleased for the first time since the reign of William the Conk. The common people, however, were ignored and faced the same dire penalties as before. The subject lay dormant for the next 170 years.

But old customs die hard and among the rural community of the country – the vast majority of the populace at that time – picking continued to play a central role in men's lives. Skills that had been acquired and refined over the centuries by these peasants, notably the development of the use of the right sleeve, were not to be easily forfeited. The Decree Nosi had driven nosepickers indoors and it was only after dark or in the privacy of their own homes that the ordinary citizen was safe to indulge himself. Even today, this centuries-old fear of 'picking in public' lingers on in many places.

Gradually, pressure grew in the shires for the repeal of the Decree Nosi. The peasants' demands went unheeded. In 1381, Simon Snyff and Nat Bogey led a band of 500 hand-picked men in a march on the capital demanding the right 'freelie and in good faithe to pluck and rolle as in ye dayes of yore whereof we yearn most loyally'. As every schoolboy knows, the uprising was put down after some fierce hand-to-hand fighting and the two ringleaders were executed by Richard II in a fit of pique.

Another eighty years passed until the matter came to a head in the Wars of the Noses. Almost overnight, nostrils flared up once again to become a political tissue.* Civil war ensued over the right of an Englishman to pick his nose in public. The two opposing sides were easily distinguishable from one another: those who were against nosepicking wore white noses; those in favour of nosepicking wore red ones.

The two sides were not reconciled for some twenty years. Peace was achieved only after a compromise was drawn up by the great statesman Warwick the Nosepicker. By this, the ordinary citizen was granted the same rights as the earls and barons on condition that:

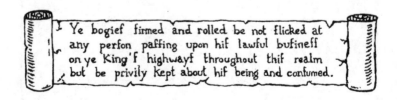

Ye bogief firmed and rolled be not flicked at any perfon paffing upon hif lawful bufineff on ye King'f highwayf throughout thif realm but be privily kept about hif being and confumed.

*Is this a misprint? (*Ed.*) No. (*R.F.*)

Leonardo's *Mona Lisa*

The Wars of the Noses, ending in the repeal of the hated Decree Nosi, coincided with an unprecedented flowering of nosepicking all over Europe. Artists like Michelangelo and Leonardo da Vinci featured it in their work.

Michelangelo's Sistine Chapel mural

By the middle of the reign of Elizabeth I, attitudes to nosepicking had become noticeably more enlightened, though the *Book of Common Prayer* (1571) enjoined all worshippers in the Catechism 'to keep [my] hands from picking and stealing'. When the Spanish Armada was sighted off the English coast on its way to invade the country, Sir Francis Drake was able to observe, without fear of prosecution: 'There is time aplenty to pick my nose and thrash the Spaniards. Aye, and that merrily with hands behind my back, forsooth!' Only a few decades earlier, such a remark would have cost him his life.

[26]

**Rolling bowls and rolling bogies –
all in a day's work for Sir Francis**

Writers felt even bolder and were encouraged in their treatment of the subject, most notably Shakespeare:

> And 'twixt his finger and his thumb he held
> A pouncet-box, which ever and anon
> He gave his nose and took't away again.

Henry IV, Part I, I, iii, 33–7

[27]

This liberal attitude prevailed in England for another fifty years, until the rise of Cromwell and the Puritans. Once again, civil war boiled up over a citizen's right to 'dig for that harmonious visitor which ever and anon gives joy anew to seek', as Milton put it so beautifully. The New Model Army was issued with helmets specifically designed to stop soldiers from engaging in 'this ungodly and unpleasante distraction'.

After the decisive Battle of Noseby (1645), there was a strict clampdown on nosepicking. Cromwell appointed the notorious Sir Roland Flick (no relation) as Nosepicker General to scour the countryside looking for offenders. Those caught and denounced were harshly treated – locked in the pillory, their hands kept within a tantalizing inch or two of their nostrils.

With the restoration of the monarchy, however, came the restoration of general nosepicking rights. Never again would they be questioned on English soil.

As for other parts of the world, it is only now, after the collapse of communism, that the full horrific details have emerged of nosepicking behind the Iron Curtain. Over succeeding decades, as the fledgling states of what was once the Soviet Union come to terms with democracy, we in the West shall doubtless receive ever more fascinating details of how picking prospered under the hard-nosed regime. Those accounts that have so far filtered through speak of unimaginable penalties incurred when any citizen dared to confront authority and pick in public. The fate of Snotsky (murdered with a blow of the dread Pick-axe, *cf.* William the Conk, Duke of Normandy) and the works of Solzhenitsyn (e.g. *The First Circle*) are enough to remind us that human beings will risk torture and imprisonment rather than forego the pleasure of nosepicking, even in sub-zero temperatures.

Snotsky

One hopes that China will follow the Soviet example before too long and abandon the restrictive practices of communism. There is much missionary work to be done on behalf of the Chinese people, for while a third of the world's population remain unable to pick their noses without fear of persecution, none of us can rest easy on our picking laurels. Imagine! Over one billion people released from bondage, as it were, able at last to scoop out their bogies and play with them in exactly the same way as we in the West do. Two billion extra hands at work! True, there will be enormous environmental problems – disposal of the inevitable Sino-bogey mountain, for instance, and technical advice on mass picking on a scale never undertaken before.

But we in the West have the experience, the teachers and the equipment. All hope is not lost: 'When the cherry blossom comes, the crane stoops for the water chestnut' is an old Chinese proverb that we would do well to bear in mind.

A late Ming woodcut showing some signs of Sino-sinus activity

America's contribution to the progress of nosepicking cannot be ignored for, although only a young country, its influence on the progress of free picking and its technique has been profound. Is there another country in the world that has so many nosepickers? Brown, yellow, black, red, white – these are only some of the immense variety of bogies that Americans pick every day.

It was Christopher Columbus who brought nosepicking to the Americas in 1492, but it was not until the arrival of the Pilgrim Fathers in 1620 that the habit took off. And it did so in a big way.

1492 – Columbus introduced nosepicking to Bermuda

The free spirits who arrived on the *Mayflower* were natural rebels who defied the English law on nosepicking and set sail for an unknown country and an uncertain future rather than live for ever a life of blocked noses and silted cilia. The habit spread west until a mere three generations later when, in 1770, the government, appalled at having a colony of nosepickers under its sovereignty, sent out troops to take the rebel pickers in hand. The Americans stood in line defiantly flicking bogies at the soldiers. In the infamous Boston Massacre which followed, five people were picked off and killed.

It was the Boston Tea Party, three years later, that led directly to the War of Independence: a group of prominent Bostonians was invited to take tea aboard an English frigate at anchor in Boston harbour.

Instead of politely drinking their Darjeeling and munching shortbread biscuits, the Bostonians sat solemnly picking the snot from their noses and eating it.

This was too much for the British and war was declared two years later. The American troops were led by General George 'I cannot tell a lie, father, I have picked my nose' Washington.

Largely thanks to him, the American Constitution expressly permits 'All you guys and dolls to geddon down now just whenever yer darn well feel like it an' stick that li'l ol' finger o' yourn up yer cotton-pickin' nose. Ah'm tellin' yer, yer hear? An' don't yer let no one tell yer differen'. Hell no. Well alright.'

Ironically, it was only two years after the American Constitution had been drawn up that the French Revolution began, with disastrous consequences for the hitherto contented, peace-loving nosepickers of France. Once again the monarchy was the catalyst. Louis XVI was one of the great nosepickers of modern times. Indeed, the French have always been among the keenest and most refined of all nosepicking nations, the Bourbon nose considered by many connoisseurs to be the very best for the purpose.

Curiously, in France it was the common people who decided that nosepicking should be abolished and who called upon the King to stop picking his nose in public. Not unnaturally the King refused. The result, as everyone knows, was the French Revolution.

Louis XVI and hundreds of other nosepickers were guillotined in an attempt to wipe out the habit in a single stroke. As had been demonstrated by the course of nosepicking in England and elsewhere, any such attempt was bound to end in failure. History had already shown that it took more than a few beheadings to stop nosepicking.

Top lot get tops lopped

With supreme irony the leader who emerged from the ruins of the revolution was one of the most notorious nosepickers in history, the original 'bogeyman', Napoleon Bonaparte.

By the time the French discovered their mistake, he had established himself in an invulnerable position. Lest the common people should discover his addiction and instigate another revolution, Bogey was begged not to pick his nose in public. This proved impossible for a man who gave his name to one of nosepicking's basic positions, the Corsican Shove (see Chapter 3). Thereupon, it was decided that his right hand should be permanently sewn into the left breast of his tunic to remove it from the path of temptation.

Thus it was that the long struggle of nosepicking, its evolution into an art form and subsequent acceptance at all levels of society throughout the world, entered its final chapter. Championed by kings, at times denied the common people, at others despised and rejected by them, this most ancient and agreeable of pastimes came at least to be accepted by all. More popular than fishing, more fun than football, not even *Coronation Street, Celebrity Big Brother* or *Neighbours* could claim to hold so many in its thrall. Yet it was not until the closing decades of the nineteenth century that the working man had at last acknowledged the right of his fellow worker to 'Pick, Lick and Flick'. There, enshrined in the Trades Union Bill of Rights (1871), is the charter for which so many had picketed over the centuries:

```
BasiCally, brothers and sisters, we shall abide by
the verdiCt given in open CounCil, to follow the
deCision implemented at grassroots level by a through
through thorough mandate of all the rank and file to
reCognise the ongoing right of every member to exCavate
at will and at any time needful to his/her CirCumstanCe
his/her nasal Cavity and in whatever manner he/she
deems appropriate to effeCtuate, beCause , quite
honestly, that is what it is all about basiCally about
at the end of the day.

                          (TuC Charter, p.57,para.5,9a,Cl.7)
```

Full picking rights achieved, we can now leave those dusty old history books behind us and get down to the business in hand – picking your nose and how to go about it.

2
Nosepicking —
Your Questions
Answered

THE following question and answer section is the result of many years' consultation and correspondence with friends and patients from all over the world. The problem pages will, I trust, dispel any lurking fears and doubts you may have about sticking your finger up your nose whenever you feel like it. The 'March of the Nosepickers' (turn to p. 119) has been adopted as the international anthem of nosepickers. Please learn it and sing it whenever you can.

Here's hoping that the old hands among you will pick up some fresh material for your hobby and that newcomers will find much to fascinate and intrigue. Welcome to the worldwide brotherhood of nosepicking. Relax, enjoy – oh, and happy hunting!

What exactly is nosepicking?

Nosepicking is, purely and simply, the technique of extracting bogies or snot from the nasal cavity (see diagrams), rolling it between thumb and forefinger into a small ball shape and then eating, wiping or flicking it.

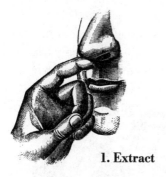

1. Extract

2. Roll

3. Flick

BASIC SKILLS OF NOSEPICKING

What is a bogey? Come to that, what is snot?

Snot is nothing more than nasal mucus, which is secreted by the nasal mucosa (the lining of the nose). It contains, perhaps surprisingly to the novice, a number of white blood cells which give it that greeny-yellowy colour. It also contains a great deal of bacteria – streptococci to give it its proper name. Snot, according to the latest medical findings, is seething with it.

Blimey.

Makes you think, doesn't it? Well, that's snot taken care of. Now, a bogey (or *mucus firmus* as we call it) is just an old, crusty piece of hardened mucus that has stuck to the inside of the nose. It's nobody's fault; no one is to blame; there should be no guilt feelings attached to discovering one up your nose. It or 'they' (depending how frequently you pick) is/are there to be taken whenever the mood comes upon you.

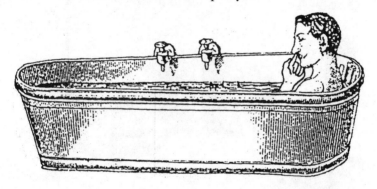

Alternatively, it is possible to advance the course of Nature and make your own bogey. This is called 'Rolling Your Own'.

What equipment do I need?

Before you start to pick your nose you should check you have the following:

(a) One thumb.

(b) One index finger (though the third finger is frequently preferred; or both together).

(c) One handkerchief (optional) or sleeve.

In the nineteenth century, nosepicking accessories were commonplace

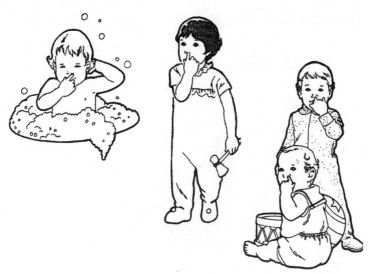

Is it difficult to pick up?

No. For most people it is simply a matter of finding the two holes at the end of your nose, waiting until a bogey has formed and then inserting the thumb and/or index finger.

However, it is always advisable to start as young as possible – two or three years old is by no means too early – as many adults find it difficult to start nosepicking later on in life. The nose needs to be flexible and the fingers nimble and accurate for a deeply satisfying experience. People in their twenties or thirties can experience real frustration when watching youngsters and senior citizens picking their noses effortlessly and with obvious pleasure.

All too often this can be traced back to lack of early nosepicking training. So do ask your father, brother or teacher for help and advice if you feel you are not getting the best out of your nose.

Is nosepicking dangerous?

In certain exceptional cases, yes. As with every pastime that is worth pursuing and perfecting, practice makes perfect but along the way, accidents, inevitably, sometimes happen.

The most common cause for concern is an increase in the size of the nostril produced by over-ambitious picking. Redness, swelling and small boils on the side of the nose are all giveaway signs of 'too much too soon'. Reduce your finger activity for a short time until the symptoms subside. Experience combined with caution and commonsense are needed to ensure a lifetime's enjoyment of nosepicking. So beware the hasty thrust – your finger can be a dangerous weapon!

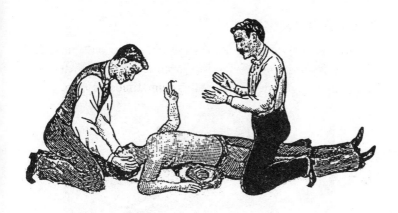

Fatal incidents have been few indeed. A tragic loss was the great Romanian nosepicker Wodsa Mewcus, who suffocated and died in 1973 during the Ceausescu Palme d'Or when both thumbs and index fingers became jammed. But, with careful training, nosepicking is no more dangerous than any other sport.

Do not pick your nose when playing a musical instrument or while using superglue. In case of emergency call the fire brigade.

Will it make me go blind?

Many adolescent boys ask this. The answer is emphatically 'No!' It may make you go cross-eyed eventually, but actual loss of vision will not occur. Nosepicking can sometimes lead to loss of appetite, when an extensive forage has taken place between meal times. (Bogey nutritional value is as high as most breakfast cereals.)

Early health campaign poster

Where can I learn to pick my nose?

Probably the best way is to learn from your father and his friends. The following general guidelines may be useful while you are picking things up:

(a) Watch carefully, but do not let the picker know he is being observed.

(b) Do not make comments while observing.

(c) Keep calm.

(d) Practise in private what you have seen in public.

(e) REMEMBER: do not become discouraged if success is not immediate. Once mastered, you will have an extra skill for life, like tying your shoelaces or riding a bicycle.

If your father is not available for instruction, watch drivers in their cars (in traffic jams or waiting at lights), policemen, traffic wardens and taxi drivers. You will pick up many handy tips from them. Once you've learned the basics, the best way for youngsters to develop the habit and become confirmed nosepickers is in the classroom or in the playground. Rolling and flicking techniques can be experimented with, and progress is usually rapid. Later, whether in warehouse, university or office, rapid gains can be made in speed and accuracy.

'Pick your moment carefully' is a good rule of thumb.

Can I ask my mum how to pick my nose?

Not unless you want a clip round the ear.

Why?

Because your mother, in common with the majority of her sex, will never admit that she has ever picked her nose.

What, never?

Not ever. At any time.

How long does it take to become an expert?

A matter of days. It will quickly become evident whether or not you are a natural nosepicker with the potential of becoming a great nosepicker – perhaps even with the chance of representing your country abroad – or whether, like most people, you will develop slowly and unconsciously into a solid, reliable nosepicker for all seasons.

When is the best time to pick my nose?

Literally any time, but particularly in front of other people. Depending on age and experience, the best places are in the classroom, during lunch and tea, on the bus, train and tube, in the office and while watching television. It is considered de rigueur to pick your nose at formal dinners, receptions, investitures and balls.

How do I produce a good bogey?

The sixty-four-thousand dollar question. See Chapter 3.

How do I know there will be something up there to pick?

Experience. A blocked nasal passage is not always an indication that a bogey is there waiting to be removed. If you have a cold, the blockage will frequently be the result of *gunge* (see Glossary of Terms), which makes collecting and rolling time-consuming and messy.

Sometimes it is possible, especially after a cigarette or being in a smoke-filled room, to feel a bogey in both nostrils. These frequently vibrate against the wall of the nasal passage on inhalation, indicating that excavation is not only available but urgently required.

If this occurs, do not delay, as a large bogey unpicked may well break loose of its own volition and either suspend itself over your upper lip or drop on to the floor.

I have often been told to 'wipe my nose'. How can I avoid this?

Don't fret. Even very experienced nosepickers have similar requests made to them. Often, after stepping from the shower or after a swim, wife, mother, partner or friend will point out to you that 'you have got something hanging from your nose'. In this situation, take the thumb and index finger, pinch the end of the nose (covering both nostrils) and, with a quick downward thrust from the wrist, flick the 'something' on to the floor. That'll teach them.

Half the fun of nosepicking is discovering the presence of a bogey. Who needs someone to point it out for you?

By the way, some of the best bogies can be found immediately after emerging from the shower. Get into the habit of making a nose check and enjoy the results at your leisure.

Apropos wiping, one of the most sophisticated methods is to pick your nose then, using the same hand, casually run your fingers through your hair. Very popular. You can always wash it out later. Only if you want to, of course.

Is nosepicking addictive?

Yes. Once you have begun, there is little that medical science can do to break the habit. If you need counselling, then NPA* is there to help twenty-four hours a day (see the *Yellow Pages* for your local branch).

Are there any organizations I can join where nosepicking is accepted?

Nosepicking is not only accepted but actively encouraged in the following places:

> The Carlton Club
> The Reading Room of the British Museum
> The Athenaeum
> The House of Commons
> The Stock Exchange

How far can I push my finger(s) up my nose?

Generally speaking, if you've pushed your fingers up so far that you can't remember your name, then you've pushed them up too far.

*Nosepickers' Anonymous.

[61]

Which finger should I use?

Another brain-teaser that geneticists and behaviourists have pondered for years. It's the old story of Nature versus Nurture. Many people divide the world into four sorts: those who use their index finger to pick (usually an incisive, purposeful personality); those who favour the little finger or 'pinkie' (for whom it is hard to avoid labels of affectation and gentility); those who use the thumb (largely, it seems, brutal, aggressive pickers, insensitive to the feelings of others); and those whose instincts incline them towards the two-digit attack (greedy, manipulative, ambitious, extrovert).

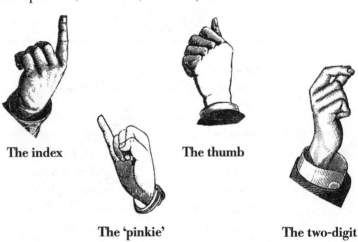

The index   The thumb

The 'pinkie'   The two-digit

If I pick my nose in bed, is it all right to wipe the bogies on the sheets?

Yes. Sure. Of course. But most people roll them up and flick them at the wardrobe to see if they can make it 'ping'. Try it in the dark, shooting 'blind'. Fun and skilful, too.

Moustaches – a help or a hindrance?

Personal preference plays a large part here. Some people like to go around with the odd bogey stuck to the bristles and wait until two or three have collected before wiping them off or eating them. This way, rolled into one, you can produce a satisfyingly large monster bogey – something to show your friends, perhaps, or make use of in an extended play session.

Alternatively, you may feel that the problems that arise when a soft bogey disintegrates in a full moustache make it an impractical proposition. Some men have been forced to shave off their moustaches, so intractable and glutinous have the bogies become. There's no doubt about it – it is more difficult to get a finger up the opening of a bushy, hair-covered nostril than up a smooth, uncluttered one. But '*Chacun à son goo*' as the French say.

If I blow my nose on a handkerchief, should I inspect what I have blown?

Again, all a matter of taste. Personally, I like to see what I've produced – the whites and many-hued greens, the odd little bubble, the occasional yellow – all make for variety and interest. To simply wrap it up sight unseen seems a waste. But why use a handkerchief?

If someone tells me off for picking my nose, what excuse can I give?

Courage, mon brave! If 'caught', turn the situation to your advantage and reply with one of the following phrases:

- 'Look at the colour/size/shape of that one, guys!'

- 'Do be quiet or the others will all want one.'

- 'Have you ever had one of those days when your nose just won't stop itching and you can't get rid of it?'

- 'How kind of you to volunteer. I'm exhausted.'

I am left-handed. Will this affect my ability to pick my nose?

Your picking ability will not be affected per se, but great care must be taken when driving a car while picking. For UK residents, mind your left hand doesn't adhere to the top of the gearstick (right hand for residents of the United States and other countries).

Can you give me some tips on looking after my fingernails?

One of the most important aspects of successful nosepicking is good manicure. It's an area to which, sometimes, even experienced pickers fail to give enough attention. Nails that are too long can nick the interior of the nasal passage, making it most uncomfortable. In extreme cases, when mining a particularly reticent specimen, the nail may be inadvertently bent back. Most painful. (See Chapter 4 for recommended nail length.)

Worse still, however, are the fingernails that have been cut or bitten too short. Here the principal tool of picking has been left with a smooth and rounded end, and the finger or thumb cannot make a purchase on the prize within. How many of us have spent fruitless hours trying in vain to retrieve a bogey using only the 'non-stick' extremity of our index finger, to end up with nothing but a stretched nose? I know I have! But seriously – do pay attention when filing and cutting your nails. You are cutting them not only for comfort but to provide the best, most efficient tool for your favourite pastime. Write it on your mirror: 'Clip, but don't snip the tip!' I'm sure this will help.

Can I pick other people's noses?

NEVER pick someone else's nose without permission. Remember the old adage:

> You can pick your nose,
> You can pick your friends,
> But you can't pick your friend's nose.

How can I get rid of ugly stains on my clothes?

Snot on cotton, linen and suede is extremely hard to remove. On suede it almost invariably leaves a permanent stain and while it may be cool for some nosepickers to proclaim their hobby in this way, the more sophisticated digger for bogies will not want to advertise his inexperience in this way. Telltale black marks on fabric are ineradicable signs to the streetwise picker that they are dealing with an amateur. If you use a sleeve, remember those dry-cleaning bills. You may find that the average high-street cleaner will take one look at a snot-embossed jacket or shirt and refuse to take it in. Specialists are few and far between, and you can end up paying through the nose.

When do you recommend the use of a handkerchief?

Only use a handkerchief as a last resort. First, of course, it is far more enjoyable to pick your nose without a handkerchief. Direct contact gives a far more satisfying experience. Second, wrapping a handkerchief round your finger (or fingers) will add enormously to the circumference of the digit(s) and make picking more difficult. Why make a tight spot tighter still?

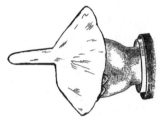

Third, bogies do not always adhere to cotton or man-made fibres. They will, however, almost always stick to your finger. Even the most recalcitrant bogey has to admit defeat when the tip of a finger hoves into view!

Lastly, a handkerchief will never be entirely clean again once it has been used for ferreting and/or blowing. Inevitably, the handkerchief with its captured bogies will lie wrapped in the warmth of your pocket for some time before it is eventually put into the wash.

This may be weeks or even months later. After this length of time, not even the strongest commercial adhesive will stick to a handkerchief like a bogey. If you insist on using a handkerchief, the following procedure for washing is recommended:

(a) Boil in caustic soda and leave to soak overnight.

(b) Scrape off residue from hankie with Stanley knife.

(c) Repeat step (a).

(d) Immerse for two days in white dye solution.

(e) Wash normally and repeat steps (a) to (e).

Avoid getting bogies on man-made fibres (dressing gowns and shirt fronts are particularly vulnerable).

Remember – 'A snappy picker is a happy picker!'

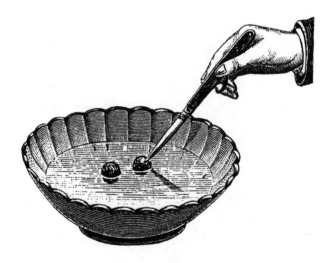

Overnight soaking often causes bogies to rise to the surface

What happens to bogies when I go swimming?

This is one of those questions that have baffled researchers and scientists for decades. There is no doubt that when you go swimming in a pool or in the sea, the amount of gunge in the nose increases dramatically. In the sea, of course, there is no detectable trace, for salt water would seem to absorb whatever we blow into it. In a public swimming pool it is different. Barrington and Coupe's masterly study of the effect of chlorine on bogies (*Spit and Spume*, Indiana University, 1984) showed conclusively that anything emanating from a swimmer's nose stayed floating in the water for up to two weeks or until the pool was emptied, whichever was the sooner. Invisible to the naked eye, the mucus that every swimmer lets go of – intentionally or otherwise – forms an integral part of the water in which we swim.

3

P.Y.O. —
The Technique
of Nosepicking

or

'Send me a postcard
when you reach the top'

F<small>IRST</small> published in 1897, Winkle's *Pictorial Rhinology* is still the standard work. Long out of print, the drawings reproduced here (courtesy of the trustees of the Victoria and Albert Museum, London) are taken from the original copper-plates by Nathan Winkle himself.

Nosepicking for Pleasure has merely added a small number of additional illustrations to demonstrate the new advances in technique made during the last century, notably Monty's Mole and the Up and Under. We hope that their inclusion will be of benefit not only to rhinologists and nosepickers, but to sociologists and social workers alike. We believe that the pictures represent the most complete collection of picking techniques yet published.

A few words of clarification may be in order to produce the best results in conjunction with these illustrations.

Nathan Winkle's illustrations were drawn for nosepicking under 'ideal conditions', that is to say when the subject has a certain amount of experience, is relaxed, and when the prevailing room atmosphere is warm without being dry. Other things to remember, detailed by Winkle in his preface, remain as true today as they did over a hundred years ago:

Timing plays an important factor – pounce at your peril.
Patience produces perfection.
Consistency = elasticity = expertise = consistency.

Monty's Mole

Up and Under

The Victoria Cross

Bristow's Shunt

The Substitute

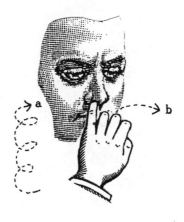

Open Inverted Standard Ballistic

The Sailor's Yarn   **Revolving Thrust and Jerk**

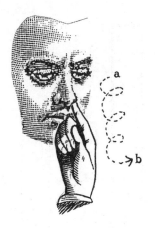

The Winkle

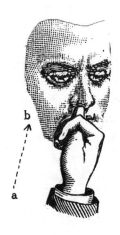

The Corsican Shove

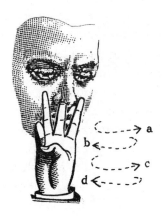

Riddle's Twist

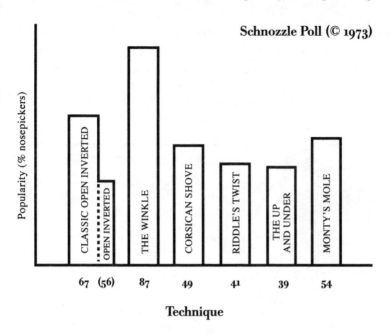

Schnozzle Poll (© 1973)

The latest survey on nosepicking (Schnozzle Poll, 1973) shows that 67 per cent of all nosepickers prefer the classic Open Inverted for a quick pick, a large proportion of whom (56 per cent) go on to flick in one continuous movement (Open Inverted Standard Ballistic). This method is not recommended for sustained picking over a long period of time, say two or three hours, when serious silting has occurred. For removing this, no fewer than 87 per cent of those questioned used the Winkle. The Corsican Shove, Riddle's Twist, the Up and Under and Monty's Mole all showed up favourably in the survey (49, 41, 39, and 54 per cent respectively).

Winkle's comprehensive study included the famous designs for an autopicker by Leonardo da Vinci and are reproduced here (courtesy of Nippahama Corporation, Japan) for the first time since 1897.

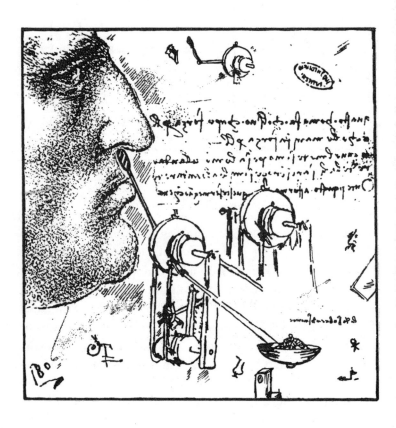

FLICKING

This most important aspect of technique, so popular today, can be great fun and provide hours of entertainment, either alone or in company. But beware! Some people still do not like having bogies flicked at them! If your target looks as though he/she may not be a fellow flicker (or if they are bigger than you), just smile at them and let them see you eat the bogey instead. They will almost always turn away. This leaves you free to quickly extract and prepare your next bogey, flick it into their hair or wipe it casually on their clothing while they are not looking. Harmless, safe and hilarious.

4
Problems
with Picking

For those who experience difficulties with nosepicking, we have selected the topics that most widely reflect your concerns from letters received by Professor Flicket.

Although I have tried for many years (I am now sixteen) I still cannot produce bogies. Is this unusual? What can I do to make them?

(M. Saint-Germain, Paris)

The answer to the first question is 'yes'. Are you sure you are inserting your fingers into the correct orifice? If you are still uncertain, please consult Chapter 3, which will confirm exactly which holes we are talking about. If you are picking the correct holes and you can find nothing, we suggest sitting in any confined space designated for the smoking of cigarettes. If that does not produce a string of bogies, nothing will.

My index finger (recommended by you as the ideal picking tool) is too big to fit up my nose. What should I use instead?

(B. H. Challoner, Bonnval)

Your pinkie. In time you will find that, with regular usage and firm manipulation, your nostrils will stretch to accommodate your index finger. I do hope so.

My boyfriend and I have a good relationship and he says that he wants to marry me. There is one problem, however, which I do not know how to tell him about. When we are making love, he leans on one elbow and starts to pick his nose. It is most off-putting and not very romantic, but how should I let him know?

(S. T., BOORMAN FALLS)

Have you tried picking your nose at the same time? Ensure both hands are free of contact with your boyfriend, lie back and pick away. You will quickly discover, as he has, that nosepicking is far more satisfying than sex.

How can I join the International Conkress of Competitive Nosepicking?

(P. BROWN, HONG KONG)

Visit the ICCN website at www.pickunlickungood.com or write to Eastgate & German, 2431 Stafford Boulevard, Milwaukee for details. The join-up fee of $10 is for life membership. Weekly bulletins, notification of worldwide nosepicking events, a lively message board, free entry to all local nose dives and a regularly updated contact list are just some of the benefits.

I my fingernails chew. This is making it most difficult extremely to get grip on the wonderful things inside my nose I know waiting are. Please have you advice?

(N. JAEGER, MÜNCHEN)

All nosepickers who chew their nails are undoubtedly making problems for themselves. We recommend a minimum of 3 mm above the fingertips for efficient and satisfying picking. (You might like to know that no less than 6 mm is the minimum laid down by the International Standing Rules on Forcible Egress, which govern competitive nosepicking.) False nails are available from all good chemists and have achieved excellent results, though there is a danger of these snapping off mid pick, so take care. Alternatively, you could ask a friend to pick your nose for you.

My girlfriend picks her nose in public even in the street and when we are having a meal. I have told her that I think it is downright disgusting and a liberty, but she takes no notice. What should I do to stop her?

(J. M. B. FRICS, STRATHCLYDE)

Move with the times. Most Americans (and, I may say, many Scotsmen, Mr Frics!) have left these old prejudices behind. They expect and, indeed, encourage their female companions to pick their noses. Like underarm hair or unshaven legs, a woman who picks her nose can be a most attractive proposition for many men. Over the past few years, girls with pale white legs that bruise easily, who wear no tights or stockings and who have a preference for white high-heeled shoes lead the way. They have shown that it is quite socially acceptable for women to pick with the rest of us. Good luck.

I suffer from an excess of nasal hair. Is there anything that can be done about this?

(I. R. PRIGIONE, ROME)

There is no reason for anybody living at the beginning of the twenty-first century to be bothered by excessive nasal hair. We have the technology and it is cheap and easy to use – in fact so easy that you can operate it yourself at home. What am I talking about? The Flicket Imperial Trimmer suitable for all unwanted hair – nose, ears, eyebrows or anywhere else. It is made of hygienic lightweight Bakelite, is easy to clean and comes with full operating instructions. No batteries required. As a special offer to readers of this book we are offering the Flicket Imperial Trimmer for just $12 (or equivalent currency) including postage and packing. (The normal retail price for this indispensable aid to facial grooming is $25!) Just send a cheque to R. F. Enterprises (Trimmer), Fabian Way, Oakley, CA 60095. If not absolutely delighted, I will offer a full refund within twenty-eight days.

The Flicket Imperial Trimmer

My husband and I have never picked our noses and have been happily married for over thirty years. Last June, though, he left me for a nosepicker half his age. My world has fallen apart and I still cannot believe it has happened. Please, what can I do to get him back?

(MRS P. COTTON, ESSEX)

I am sorry to hear of your domestic problems, Mrs Cotton, but I am sure you will not be surprised at the advice I shall give to you – the same that I give everybody in a similar situation. Don't delay, start picking today! Only then will you have a chance of winning back your man.

5
A Fun
Fact File
for Pickers

WHICH TYPE ARE YOU?

Match your nose to one of these nose types.

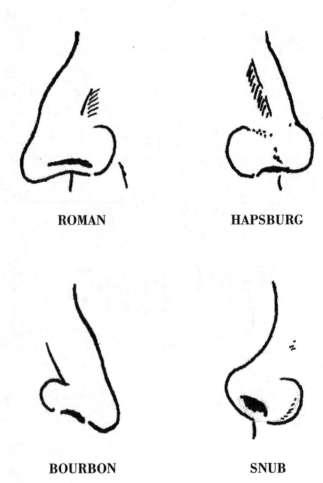

ROMAN   HAPSBURG

BOURBON   SNUB

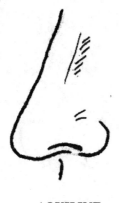

AQUILINE

RETROUSSÉ

GREEK

COAL MINER

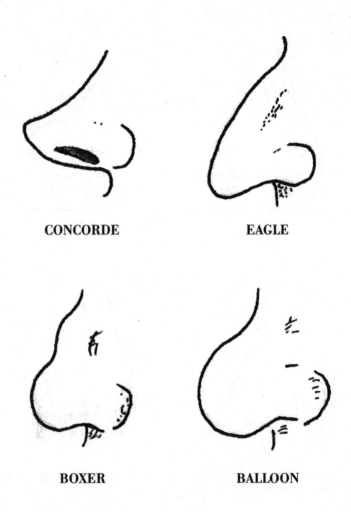

CONCORDE   EAGLE

BOXER   BALLOON

GREAT NOSES PAST AND PRESENT

Match these noses with their famous owners. Were they born with them, or did they shape them themselves?

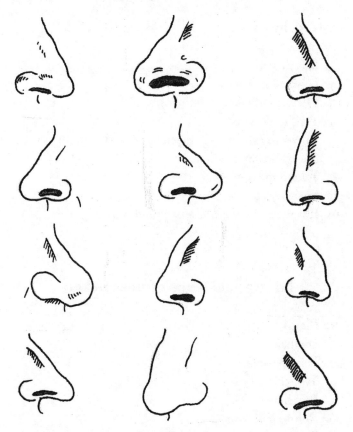

Barbra Streisand	Duke of Wellington	Frederick the Great
Edith Sitwell	Julius Caesar	Barry Manilow
Bob Hope	Jimmy Durante	Maria Callas
Napoleon Bonaparte	Roland Flicket	King Faisal

LEAGUE TABLES

Highest incidence of nosepickers

1. Taxi drivers
2. Sales reps
3. Bus drivers
4. Football players
5. Customs officials
6. Traffic wardens
7. University students (especially those belonging to evangelical movements)
8. Telephone operators
9. Sociologists
10. Royal watchers (*Sun, Mirror* and *Star*)

Lowest incidence of nosepickers

1. Pianists
2. Dentists
3. Hairdressers
4. Typists
5. Butchers
6. Refuse collectors
7. Television newsreaders
8. Archbishops (in public)
9. Members of the Royal Family (in public)
10. Surgeons

6
Nostrildamus — Your Future in the Stars

PROPHETS and fortune-tellers down the centuries have used the stars and planets, crystal balls, tea leaves and tarot cards to predict the future, but it was the sixteenth-century mystic Nostrildamus (1503–66) who foresaw the rise of Hitler, the assassination of the Kennedy brothers and other world-shattering events while picking his nose and reading the astrological chart.

Apart from the writings of Nostrildamus and updated especially for this volume by famed ball-gazer Bram Tatorus ('Seer To The Stars') of the *Los Angeles Argus*, this summary will enable you to tell at a glance under which sign of the zodiac the nosepicker sitting opposite you was born. Is he/she your type? Are you compatible? Your future could be in the palm of someone's hand.

Hi there nostril-gazers!
Bear in mind the salient points of each zodiac sign's characteristics and you'll find this to be an invaluable guide to dating and mating. Compatibility and common interests make for good relationships; add to this the shared joy of nosepicking – the right sort of nosepicking that suits you both – and your future happiness is assured.

Have a good day and lots of GREAT tomorrows!
'Sin-seer-ly' yours,

Bram Tatorus

Nostrildamus

ARIES (The Ram)

21 March–20 April

Aries is governed by its ruling planet Mars, the god of war. Not surprising then that the most noticeable characteristic of the Arian nosepicker is the aggression with which he plunges his index finger up the nostril and forces a result. He does not care where or when he picks his nose nor if doing so makes him unpopular with others – he'll just carry right on doing it. Quick rule of thumb: Aries often has a sore, red nose.

Famous Arian nosepickers include Otto von Bismarck and Adolf Hitler.

TAURUS (The Bull)

21 April–22 May

Physically, Taurus is the best equipped of all the signs for nosepicking. He is generally short and broad; though the size of his fingers may cause him problems, his nose is also wide. In short, there's plenty of it and it's easy to get at. His temperament, too, helps him. Patient and practical Taurus takes time and pains over what he picks and how he does it. Does that fingernail being prised out slowly and carefully belong to a Taurean? Why not see if you're right? Just go over and ask!

Karl Marx, one of history's great nosepickers, was a Taurus.

GEMINI (The Twins)
22 May–21 June

Gemini's ruling planet is Mercury, which makes anyone born under this sign a quick thinker and highly resourceful. You won't find a Gemini missing out on the opportunity for a furtive burrow! Queuing for food in the canteen, buying a theatre ticket or trying on a new pair of shoes – if there's a bogey there, Gemini will go for it, quickly and expertly, before you can say 'Jack Robinson'. Gemini, the twin, often lives a double life and, if he's spotted having a surreptitious pick, will cleverly disguise the fact or respond with a lightning-fast excuse, e.g. 'Gosh, my nose is itchy today.'

Queen Victoria and George V were Geminis.

CANCER (The Crab)
22 June–22 July

You can spot a Cancer nosepicker a mile off. They always leave it too late and by the time they start ferreting around, the likelihood is that the bogey has become far too encrusted and hard. Result? Cancer the Crab has his claws stuck up his nose for far too long – turning away into a corner or hiding his face behind a handkerchief, he chips and picks away in the vain hope that no one has noticed. Of course, everyone has. Ruled by the Moon, the sign of Cancer has an affinity with water and the sea. You'll find that many divers, sailors, fishermen and lighthouse keepers pick their noses in this way.

Two famous Cancerians were Julius Caesar and the Duke of Windsor.

LEO (The Lion)
23 July–23 August

Does any sign of the zodiac enjoy nosepicking more than Leo? I doubt it. The life and soul of the party, there he'll be, shovelling prawn crackers into his mouth with one hand and stuffing his bogies in with the other. It's done with such lovable gusto, so unselfconsciously, that you can't help warming to him at once. The extrovert Leo can be spotted doing wonderfully imaginative things with his bogies – pulling them out like an elastic band, rolling them up into little balls, tossing them in the air and catching or kicking them as they come down. Great nosepickers to be with if you're just starting off. Many actors and politicians are Leo.

Mussolini was a notable example of a Leo nosepicker gone wrong.

VIRGO (The Virgin)
24 August–23 September

Meticulous Virgo puts all the other zodiac signs to shame when it comes to efficient, precise picking. You won't find Virgo with a bogey up his nose for long: cleanliness and orderliness are the chief characteristics of the sign and as soon as there's something there, out it comes! Not that Virgo rushes. No, he wants the best every time – not too hard, not too runny – for the Virgoan search for perfection means that he very rarely has his finger out of his nose, always on the lookout for that ideal lump of snot. Being critical, a Virgo will generally inspect any bogey carefully before disposing of it. Compatible signs are Capricorn, Taurus or a fellow Virgo.

Leo Tolstoy, Peter Sellers and President Lyndon B. Johnson were all born under this sign.

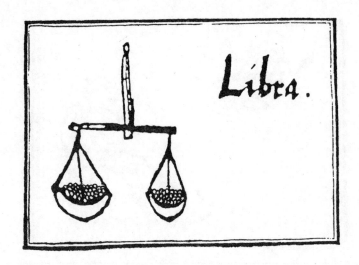

LIBRA (The Scales)
24 September–23 October

Libra, it must be admitted, is not the ideal nosepicker. He avoids conflict and dislikes upsetting people. If there's a bogey in the offing and it's 'not quite the right time' to do something about it, then, rather than risk annoyance he will let it remain there. The sign is also noted for laziness and often you will find that the person opposite you with a bogey up his nose is a Libran: he simply can't be bothered to pick it. Librans are not known for their love of rough manual work, but they make good sculptors and interior designers, so perhaps there is some hope for them yet. Probably not a good plan to date a Libran if you are a confirmed nosepicker. You will find little in common.

Lord Nelson was a Libra and so was Pope Paul VI.

SCORPIO (The Scorpion)
24 October–22 November

Many writers have commented on the Scorpio's ability to 'cut, penetrate and probe'. It is, in many ways, the ideal nosepicking sign for not only do they enjoy this characteristic of obsessive digging, constantly trying to unearth the hidden and reveal the forgotten, but they also have a tenacity and persistency that leads many of them to spend much of their working day with fingers firmly entrenched up their nasal orifices. And, my, how they go about it! The energy and concentration they bring to rooting out even the smallest deposit is heartening to witness. Scorpios, traditionally, make good surgeons and soldiers, explorers and leaders. What more does one need to become a nosepicker?

Both Martin Luther and General de Gaulle were Scorpios, as is confirmed by their portraits.

SAGITTARIUS (The Archer)
23 November–21 December

In terms of frequency you are most likely to spot a Sagittarius at work. Sagittarians cannot bear to be tied down anywhere. Hence the phenomenon of the 'picker on the move' (so memorably filmed by Jacques Tati in his classic movie *Traffic*). Company reps, travelling salesmen, taxi drivers, lorry drivers, bus drivers, airline pilots and air hostesses – the chances are they'll be Sagittarian nosepickers. Their boisterous natures can make them irritating picking companions at times. They are the ones who go over the top, flicking bogies at other people, wiping them on their friends' clothes and hair – and laughing uproariously. Choose their company with caution.

Did you know Winston Churchill, Ludwig van Beethoven and Walt Disney were all Sagittarians?

CAPRICORN (The Goat)
22 December–20 January

Can you imagine a sign that genuinely doesn't enjoy nosepicking? Well, Capricorn is that sign. Although Capricorn produces as many bogies as the next person and knows that somehow or other they will have to be removed, there is no enthusiasm for the task. Picking is done mechanically, reticently and reluctantly. The end result will be the same – a fingertip covered with snot – but this won't appeal to or interest Capricorn one iota. Somehow they can only rarely enter into the fun of the thing and make the most of it.

William Gladstone and Joan of Arc were both born under this sign.

AQUARIUS (The Water Carrier)
21 January–19 February

The Aquarian takes his nosepicking seriously. This is no surprise for his inventive mind loves to experiment and discover new ways of doing things. Hence, many of the far-reaching picking methods have, it is no coincidence, been perfected by Aquarians (e.g. Riddle's Twist, Monty's Mole, see Chapter 3). With his scientific bent and somewhat solemn attitude to life, it is probably Aquarius sitting opposite you on the bus examining, with unusual closeness, the deposit he has just extracted. Laugh if you will at the apparently clumsy way he uses, say, the fourth finger of his left hand to educe the bogey from his upper right nostril, but try it yourself and you will take your hat off to ingenious Aquarius.

Charles Dickens was an Aquarian and so was Frederick the Great of Prussia.

PISCES (The Fish)
20 February–20 March

What a contrast to the military efficiency of the Virgo nosepicker, or the wild enthusiasm of the Leo. Pisces lives in a daydream unaware of himself and his surroundings – he's the one with the runny nose who's forgotten to bring a handkerchief. He's the one who solves the problem by simply wiping it on his sleeve or on someone else's. Blissfully unaware of what he has in store, Pisces leaves it to others to tell him. Pisces can pick and dig with the best when the opportunity is pointed out to him, but one wishes sometimes he would wake up and show a little more initiative and *savoir faire* instead of relying on others.

Albert Einstein was, not surprisingly, a Piscean, and so was Buffalo Bill.

7
Nosepicking
in Art

Here we see some fine examples of nasal exploration as depickted by the masters ...

Edvard Munch (1863–1944)

Vincent Van Gogh (1853–90)

Henri Toulouse-Lautrec (1864–1901)

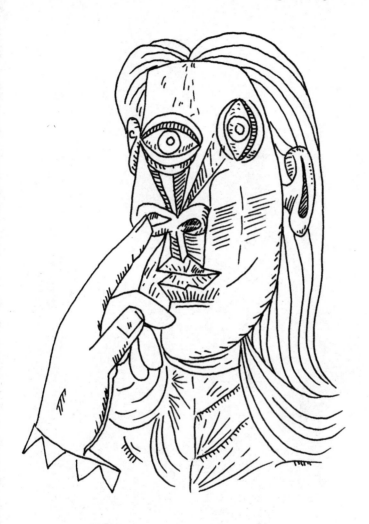

Pablo Pickasso (1881–1973)

8
Nosepicking in Verse and Song

The boy stood in the witness-box
Picking his nose like fury,
Rolling it up in little balls
And flicking it at the jury.

W E all know that famous old nursery rhyme, of course, but the pleasures of nosepicking have been celebrated for centuries in verse and song. There's that lovely ballad from the early 1900s 'God gave her a beautiful face, but she picked her nose herself' and the stirring march, beloved of all nosepickers, 'Colonel Bogey'. The tradition continues today with such pop songs as 'Everybody's doing it, doing it, doing it / Picking their nose and chewing it, chewing it.'

Here are some other old favourites. How many do you remember?

'The Sound of Mucus', JULIE ANDREWS
'Blowing in the Wind', BOB DYLAN
'Rudolph the Red-Nosed Reindeer', GENE AUTRY
'Concrete and Clay', UNIT 4 + 2
'Does Your Chewing Gum Lose Its Flavour on the Bed-Post Overnight?', LONNIE DONEGAN
'Shake, Rattle and Roll', BILL HALEY & THE COMETS
'God Only Nose', THE BEACH BOYS
'Dizzy Fingers', ZEZ CONFREY
'Hush, Hush, Hush, Here Comes the Bogey Man', HENRY HALL
'Rubber Ball', BOBBY VEE
'Second-Hand Nose', BARBRA STREISAND
'We Can Work It Out', THE BEATLES
'Teddy Bears' Picknic', HENRY HALL
'The Yellow Nose of Texas', MITCH MILLER
'It Snot Unusual', TOM JONES

MARCH OF THE NOSEPICKERS
Words and Music: Adam Zachary Flicket

When you've got an idle moment
There's a special little place,
Somewhere you can take yourself to –
It's the middle of your face.

Go on, pick your nose in public!
Why not give yourself a treat?
Don't inhale it, just descale it
While you're walking down the street.
Why wait till you're somewhere private?
Then the moment will have passed.
You want to do it! Go on, chew it!
Nail your colours to the mast!

Standing on the corner, sitting in a chair,
Watching television, why should people care?
Driving in the motor, waiting for a bus,
Why does everybody kick up such a fuss?

There's no nasal-picking season,
It goes on throughout the year.
No need to plan when you trepan to
Keep the airways clear.
Once you've got into the habit,
It's a tricky one to break.
Uncontrolled, you'll find you're sold on
Using all your fingers like a rake.

Go on, pick your nose in public!
Why not give yourself a hand?
Pick it, lick it, roll and flick it,
Stretch it like a rubber band!
There are well-intentioned people
Whom this habit will repel.
They insist this orifice is
Not to pick but smell.

Why say it's anti-social to go and pick your nose?
Why be like all the others who only pick their toes?
Marzipan or nougat, nothing can compare
With the home-produced equivalent of
chocolate éclair.

Excavating in your nostrils
Doesn't need a handkerchief.
Use your finger! It will bring a
Feeling of intense relief.
Go on! Pick your nose in public!
Quarry, mine and trawl,
Extract and winkle – in a twinkle
You will have a ball!

March Of The Nosepickers

Words and Music : Adam Zachary Flicket

When you've got an i-dle mo-ment There's a spe-cial lit-tle place, Some-where you can take your-self to – It's the mid-dle of your face.

1. Go on, pick your nose in pub - lic!
   Why wait till you're some - where pri - vate?
2. Go on, pick your nose in pub - lic!
   There are well in - ten - tioned peo - ple

Why not give your - self a treat?_____
Then the mo - ment will have passed._____ You
Why not give your - self a hand?
whom this ha - bit will re - pel.

Don't in - hale it,
want to do it!
Pick it, lick it,
They in - sist this

Nosepicking for Pleasure

just de - scale it While you're walk - ing down the street._____
Go on, chew it! Nail your
roll and flick it, Stretch it like a rub - ber band!
or - i - fice is not to

co - lours to the mast. Stand - ing on the cor - ner,
pick_____ but_____ smell. Why say it's an - ti - so - cial to

sit - ting in a chair, Watch - ing tel - e - vis - ion, why should peo - ple
go and pick your nose? Why be like all the o - thers who on - ly pick their

care? Dri - ving in the mo - tor, wait - ing for a bus,
toes? Mar - zi - pan or nou - gat, no - thing can com - pare With the

Why does ev - ery bo - dy kick up such a fuss? 1. There's no na - sal pick - ing
home pro - duced e - qui - va - lent of choc - o - late é - clair. Once you've got in - to the
2. Ex - ca - va - ting in your

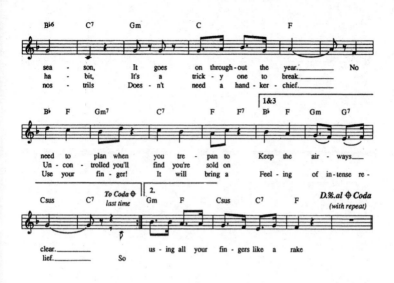

Glossary
of Terms

Words in *italics* are found elsewhere in the glossary.

Blowing
Expelling excess *snot* from the *nose* by a sudden and strong
exhalation. Footballers and council workmen have mastered
the art of holding the bridge of the *nose* between the inverted
index finger and *thumb* for highly effective results.

Bogey (pl. **bogies**)
The finished product before being flicked, rolled or eaten.

Cosa Nostril
Like the Mafia, only into organized slime.

Gouge
Sticking an *index finger* and *thumb* up your nose to get a
bogey.

Gunge
Over-production of *snot*.

Handkerchief (abbr. **hanky**)
A square (approx. 30 × 30 mm) of white or coloured cotton
used to wipe or blow the *nose*. Now obsolete.

Hands
The backs of these are used for wiping away excess *gunge* and
snot.

Index finger
The nosepicker's biggest friend. You should have two.

Mucus firmus
A technical term (Latin derivation) which, loosely translated,
means bogey.

Nose
The bit that sticks out in the middle of your face.

Pick
Sticking a finger up your *nose* to get a *bogey*.

Pinkie
Your smallest finger(s). A useful substitute for the *index finger* and much favoured by lady pickers.

Rolling
Rubbing the end of the *index finger* and *thumb* together with some *snot* on them, in order to produce a *bogey*.

Sniffing
Sharp inhalation through the *nose*. Frowned on by the International Conkress (see section on Problems).

Snot
The semi-liquid green stuff that's waiting up there.

Tati
As in 'Jacques Tati' or 'doing a Tati' or 'Have you seen that sequence in *Traffic* where everyone's picking their *noses* in their cars?' As in 'Have you put that bit in your book?'

Thumb
Used in conjunction with the *index finger* (see above) as a lever and scraper. Most pickers have two.

Wiping
Removing excess *snot* from the *nose*, mouth, hair, jumper, friend's face etc. by the use of the sleeve, or back of the hand.